THE MAGNIFICENT KEYS TO PERSONAL SUCCESS

An essential guide to mattering and fulfillment

JOHN IFAKA, Ph.D.

The Magnificent Keys To Personal Success

DEDICATION

To my loving mother and teacher, Mrs. Margaret Aina Ifaka for educating and inspiring me to succeed.

CONTENT

ACKNOWLEDGEMENT

The Author acknowledged the works of others were consulted in shaping the ideas captured in this book. They were mentioned in several parts of the work where the ideas they presented were significant.

I appreciate Frank Emmanuel and Ibrahim Momoh for their role in shaping and influencing the line of thinking expressed in this work.

Chapter One

PDMT

Success validates the meaning you can get out of existence. It becomes magnificent if you approach success from a position of power, strength, and deliberation. The magnificent path to success applies the essential keys of Purpose, Determination, Money, and Time (PDMT). Success is an elusive concept unless it is predetermined. It, therefore, means that success is set against some specific standards that a person seeks to acquire or attain. Why would a person want to set specific standards before attaining them? Without these *specific standards*, it would be difficult to *plan* and *act* towards *achieving* the *results* expected. What *success* means is that a person must have *specific standards* he *anticipates* achieving in advance before he would be required to *plan* the strategy needed to act to get the expected results. Plans are designed to get results. These results are measured against some specific standards.

The specific standard is PURPOSE. It is the end of what a plan is designed to achieve. Without a purpose, there is no need for a plan and action required to get the result. Success is measured by meeting some specific standard or purpose. The number one key to success is to always have a purpose. The purpose is predetermined in advance. The purpose is the end of a plan. Unless you have a purpose, you want to achieve, you cannot begin to design a plan. You need to search for it within you to find what you were internally built to solve. All purposes are assignments designed to solve problems.

Your purpose is unique, specifically assigned to you. You cannot fail in your purpose. If you can search for and discover it. Every individual is assigned a given purpose and a problem to solve better than others. Discovering your purpose and fulfilling it is the most importance measure of success in life.

Your purpose has provision or resources that will fund your

action toward solving the problems you were assigned to solve for humanity. The tool required to drive your purpose is your passion. Your passion is compensated in money. Your purpose is measured against the resources, compensation, or money you receive in fulfilling the purpose. Your purpose will enrich you beyond mere surviving. Your purpose resources are manifested in the range between satisfaction and self-actualization. The resources are significantly measured in money. The second magnificent key to success is the determination to develop a plan of action and follow it to competition. The third magnificent key to success is to explore the secret of money and attract an abundance of it.

The fourth magnificent key to success is the management of time. Time is essential to success. Adequate or prompt timing is a prerequisite to achieving success. Failures are associated with procrastination. Acting on a definite purpose, with the required resources and exact timing are the combined magnificent keys to success. In the following chapters, each of the magnificent keys was explored in the following order; **Purpose, Determination, Money, and Time (PDMT).**

Chapter Two

17 DIMENSIONS OF PURPOSE

A purpose is hidden but requires to be discovered before it can manifest into success. Its manifestation is revealed through its dimensions. Unless the dimensions are searched after, a purpose cannot be discovered. It is the searching for these dimensions that can bring forth the evidence of purpose. Let us now explore these dimensions, so that we can find our purpose to become successful. To discover a definite life purpose, Dennis P. Kimbro said you must answer the ultimate question of *where are you going.*

Finding your purpose is the starting point of all achievement. Robert F. Kennedy affirmed that the purpose of life is to contribute in some way to making things better and Criss

Jami concluded by saying that what matters most in life is to find a purpose to serve and make a meaningful contribution to the lives of others.

Our search for purpose is principally to understand our essence which is revealed to us through the diverse manifestation of our being. If you know the expressions of these various dimensions, you will connect them to your purpose. Purpose is here expressed as the ultimate and magnificent path to personal success. No one can succeed without knowing the definite purpose. These dimensions are a revelation to the definiteness of purpose.

I. ***Purpose is connected to your Dream.***

Your Purpose is connected to your dream. your purpose is framed, sketched, or outlined by a dream. A dream is an inward revelation or disclosure of purpose. It is inbuilt in you. You carry your purpose from your birth throughout your life. You were born with unlimited greatness deposited in your mind. It is your purpose. It is a dominant force inside you always seeking to be expressed. Most people limit dreams only to mental movie encounters during sleep. It is just a small part of it. Conscious daydreaming is the big stuff of life.

Edger Allen Poe typified this when he accounted that 'those who dream by the day are cognizance of many things which escape those who dream only at night'. Steven Spielberg incarnated the same conviction by stressing that 'I don't dream at night, I dream all day. I dream for a living. Oscar Wilde captures the same view by stating: 'Yes, I am a dreamer. For a dreamer is one who finds his way by moonlight and sees the dawn before the rest of the world do so'.

You will never succeed without a dream; your purpose is hidden in your dream. When you dream, it is specifically for a purpose. The dream I am requesting you to dream is conscious daydreaming. It is programming your purpose for you to take off. Your programming is your frame of reference. Your mind only works with your frame of reference. Big-picture thinking is equivalent to dreaming. As long as you must think and dream to be wealthy and successful, dream or think big.

Brian Tracy asserts that 'all successful men and women are big dreamers. They imagine what their future could be, ideal in every respect, and then work every day toward their distant vision, that goal or purpose'. Woodrow Wilson proclaimed the same when he stated that 'we grow great by dreams. All big men are dreamers. Eleanor Roosevelt followed the same line of reasoning by affirming that the future belongs to those who believe in the beauty of their dreams. Poter Reese was blunt with this when he insisted that dreams are only foolish to those who lack them.

Brian Tracy uttered if you can dream it, you can do it. Your limits are all within yourself. William Arthur Ward professed that if you can imagine it, you can create it. If you can dream it, you can become it. Orison Swett Marden acknowledged that all men who have achieved great things are great dreamers. Dale Carnegie proudly stated that you must love your dream to live it; people rarely succeed unless they have fun in what they are doing. Henry David Thoreau avowed that if one advances confidently in the direction of his dreams and endevour to live the life which he imagined, he will meet with success unexpected in common hours.

You were created to dream and doing so in partnership with the creator is one of His greatest gifts to you. Your purpose is connected to your dream. Live it to the realization of your contribution.

II. ***Purpose gives meaning and fulfillment***

Purpose gives meaning and fulfillment. Purpose precedes your existence. It is the WHY of your life. It is the reason why you were created. Your purpose gives meaning and fulfillment to your life. For your purpose to be meaningful, it must be clear, specific, simple, definite, consistent, and single. John D. Rockefeller presaged that 'singleness of purpose is one of the chief essentials for success in life. Vince Lombardi in the same trace commits that no matter what maybe one's aim, success demands singleness of purpose.

It is assigned to man by divinity. It carries the meaning of our existence. We have been called for a unique purpose. Every man's purpose is different and important to humanity. Everyman is on a rescue mission for humanity. Our purpose is to influence the earth with the gift of passion deposited inside us.

Life is a journey of purpose. It is not an aimless wandering exercise. In our different journeys, we have been assigned to a specific destination from where we are. The purpose is to get to know your destination and how to fulfill a given assignment. Success is getting to your destination and completing your assignment. It is the fulfillment of your purpose that gives meaning to your life.

Purpose is selflessness. It is donating your life to the cause of humanity. Ralph Waldo Emerson captured this vividly by declaring that the purpose of life is not to be happy, it is to be useful, to be honourable, to be compassionate, and to have it make some difference that you have lived and lived well.

Purpose is different from ambition. Purpose is man's contribution to humanity while ambition is man's desire for his advancement. Dennis P. Kimbro in What Makes the Great Great captured this by stating that man is here for the sake of other men only…We are here for the sake of serving others only. And only to the extent of serving others will we know our purpose of living.

Most people go through life not discovering and expressing their purpose. Their lives lack meaning because their contribution to humanity is not felt. Everyman influences the world with his purpose. If your purpose is not known, then your life is lost. The value of life is not in its duration but in its donation. What are you contributing to humanity? All greatness is hidden in purpose. No purpose is small. Washington Irving draws our attention to this fact when he stated that great minds have a purpose, and others have wishes.

III. ***Purpose reveals your identity***

Your purpose reveals your identity. By your assignment, your identity is revealed. You are what you do repeatedly. Aristotle once said that 'we are what we repeatedly do, excellence then is not an act but a habit. Every of your action is birthed from your thought and your thought is programmed response to your purpose. Your purpose carries an unwritten tag of who you are. It specifies your job description on the earth. Thomas Merton described this fact clearly by expressing If you want to identify me, ask me not where I live, or what I like to eat, or how I comb my hair, but ask me what I am living for, in detail, ask me what I think is keeping me from living fully for the thing I want to live for.

The first man was named Adam by the creator- God. The meaning of Adam is EARTH. Man was made from the earth and named after it. Cliff Goins captured a significant fact about man's mandate in his book, Stop Digging. Cliff exposes that the creator named Adam '-Earth' to identify man with his purpose and his inheritance.

The earth, therefore, is man's identity, purpose, and inheritance. God did not just make and created man on the earth, HE created everything man needed in abundance and asked Adam to call them by the name he desired. Man was given freedom from creation and was also given the mandate to govern the earth. When God created man, he placed him in a garden. This means God gave Adam an orderly place and an example of his purpose. All purposes are pre-established toward order. You have the freedom to find your purpose and establish order from it. Your purpose is to create order in the earth. Find your purpose and live it. Your purpose has your identity.

IV. ***Purpose Expresses Passion.***

Purpose expresses passion. The easiest way to find your purpose is to locate your passion. Passion is the vehicle through which you express your purpose. Passion is your hunger, thirst, or desire to fulfill your purpose. Your purpose is your assignment. It involves getting from where you are to where you want to be. It is filling a need for humanity. It is giving your priceless freedom to humanity. It is doing what you love to pursue a valuable cause that you strongly believe in. Passion is the energy or power that carries you toward the fulfillment of your purpose. The mastery of your passion is significant in the pursuit of your purpose.

Dale Carnegie avowed that 'people rarely succeed unless they have fun in what they are doing. Passion keeps you going towards the fulfillment of your purpose even when there is no possibility of reward. Passion is just fun you enjoy while doing your work. It is the fulfillment that matters to your heart. Success is not the key to happiness. Happiness is the key to success. If you love what you are doing, you will be successful. Passion creates persistence. If you have passion for your work, you won't even need encouragement to sail through difficult or troubling times; you just go to the finishing line where the reward is.

It is not luck that matters but passion when you are pursuing your purpose. Passion is the fire that ignites your spirit even when you are thinking of giving up. With passion, there is no turning back. If you love your work, your work becomes your play. Passion is what takes you out of your bed in the morning and returns you late in the evening but you still feel happy to do the same thing over and over again.

Most people give up very close to getting to their success because they lack the passion to sustain their will. You just have to feed your passion and live your purpose to create extreme wealth and great success. Mark Twain put it simply this way: work like you don't need the money. Love like you have never been hurt. Dance like nobody is watching.

Dr. Mike Murdock in his book Secrets of the Richest Man Who Ever Lived revealed that passionate people become powerful, generate enthusiasm, create waves of favour, and stay focused. However, passionate people are alert and driven solely by their inner deeper convictions rather than by the demands of their environment. This is fundamentally why they always emerge leaders and pathfinders in their endevours.

V. ***Purpose Create Expectation.***

Purpose creates expectation. All purposes are to influence and serve humanity. Purpose reveals the future and the benefits inherent in it. Those people who possess purpose and work towards it shape the direction of society. If you discover your purpose, and create a vision out of your passion and purpose in clear and specific detail, then you have the big picture of the future in front of you.

If you vividly see the future in advance, like the man who saw tomorrow, then your expectation is before you only waiting for you to take it. If you see it, manifesting it is easy. Whatever you expect is always before you. Great expectation always leads to great achievements.

What do you expect from life? There is always a provision in your purpose. See it and get hold of it. What you expect, you attract to your life. The law of expectation and the law of attraction is significantly working in the same direction with the same principle to benefit you. The law of expectation is bringing to you what you are expecting from the universe and the law of attraction is a behavioral consequence of how you act while expecting your thought to manifest. When you expect, you are consequently attracting what you are expecting. Ask yourself the following questions.

a) What am I expecting to achieve from my purpose?

b) How much money I am expecting from my purpose?

c) What am I expecting from my career, family, and health?

Always define your expectation and write it down; for there is the definiteness of purpose, what you see every day is your expectation.

Expectation motivates. Motivation is the inner drive to

pursue your purpose. Let your expectation be the reason to drive your success in life. Let your expectation be your inner drive to make the journey of your purpose. Let it drive you to your destiny. Become a winner with your expectation. Brian Tracy conveyed that winners make the habit of manufacturing their positive expectations in advance of the event.

Margaret Atwood expressed this clearer by stating that what am I living for and what I am dying for is the same question.

VI. ***Purpose precedes Vision.***

Purpose precedes vision and vision is created from purpose. Purpose provides the big picture, the expectation, and the reward of your passion. Everything about your purpose is located in your vision. Your vision is to see the destination of your purpose. Vision is the eye of purpose. Without vision, you cannot see the road to your purpose. You will be blind to your purpose.

Many people fail in life because they are visionless. They are purpose blind. How do you get to where you don't see? Everything you expect or seek comes from your vision. Imagination is the creative power of vision. Before anything can be created you must first see it. Vision is the power of the mind that connects the invisible world and the visible world. If you can see anything in the invisible world, you can hold it in the visible world. Without vision, there is no purpose because you cannot see.

Vision is the eye of the mind. It takes the mind through the route that it will use to get to the destination of its purpose- the future. Many intelligent people including scholars confuse vision for purpose. If you scan through works of literature, you will discover that both purpose and vision are used interchangeably but they are not the same. This confusion even among scholars results from our many miseries. They are closely connected but they are distinct, interconnected, and interdependent.

Purpose is uniquely different from vision. Purpose is the original intention of your existence. It is the reason for your existence. It precedes your vision. Purpose is firmly established outside vision; whether you are conscious of it or not, the purpose of your existence is always available.

You are the product of a super-intelligent being- the Infinite Intelligence. HE is the Alpha and Omega. HE created the earth, made you from it, and created you to dominate it. HE fixed your timing and place it in it. HE assigned you your purpose. Your purpose is a programme to influence the earth with your passion. Your passion is the instrument with which your difference is established. Your purpose is programmed in your mind. Your purpose is instruction. Your passion is the code of the programming on how you will manifest the instruction to fulfill your purpose. Your purpose is in your mind's memory.

Your purpose is interdependent on your vision. Your purpose is the programming of your life. Your vision's job is to locate your purpose in your mind. It searches for it and reveals your purpose by giving you a playback of your purpose. Your vision becomes the location of the big picture or destination of your life. It magnifies and transforms to see where and how you can reach your destination.

Your purpose carries your blueprint. Your blueprint is an excellent manual of your passion. Even without vision, your passion is expressing your purpose but it's like applied energy without direction. The energy dissipates aimlessly without purpose. It is the vision that shows the pathway through which your passion travels to reach the big picture. Purpose is the future and is only a vision that can see the future. What you see is manifesting towards you.

Your mind is a purpose-fulfilling machine. It is a playback machine for your purpose. Your life is stored in your purpose as a memory in your mind. Its programming is following the instruction assigned to it. If you have not discovered your purpose, your vision is blocked and you are wandering outside your instruction. You can reprogramme your purpose through the expression of your passion. In most cases, feeding your true passion is a prelude to finding your purpose. Your passion is always aligned with your purpose. If you ignore your passion, vision, and your purpose, you are operating without a compass. Never find yourself without a compass.

Your purpose – programme carries your beginning (birth) and End (Completion of your purpose). The end of a thing is always greater than the beginning. It is the completion of your purpose that brings fulfillment to your life, wealth and success is just the reward for fulfilling your purpose.

VII. ***Purpose has agenda***

Purpose has agenda. The agenda of your purpose is to enrich you beyond the satisfaction of your needs; it is specifically to enrich humanity. Your purpose has provisions. Your job is to follow the instruction of the programming of your purpose and the provision installed inside your passion will greatly manifest. Your purpose fully relies on your passion to get fulfillment. Wealth is located in your purpose. That is why it is your purpose. Your purpose has agenda. The agenda of your purpose is to enrich you to influence humanity.

Purpose is always hidden, waiting for you to discover it. Focus on your passion and you are looking at your purpose. Your passion is a vehicle of unlimited wealth. Anytime you express your passion, you are fulfilling your purpose and you are entering wealthy places. Your passion is a clue to your purpose. Locate your passion and your wealth, then success is guaranteed.

Everything you will ever be, do and have is all hidden in your passion. If you feed your passion, you are living your purpose. Until you influence the earth with your passion, you are yet to TAP into your purpose. Everyman who becomes wealthy and successful has mastered his passion and is using it to enrich the earth. Remember, man was made from the earth; he must satisfy his mandate of fruitfulness, multiplying, replenishing, subduing, and dominating the earth. When you do this, you are satisfying and fulfilling your purpose and destiny.

VIII. **Purpose defines Value**

Purpose defines value. Value is the standard measure of expectation. Value means the important stuff in your life. Value guides every decision and direction of our lives. Your purpose produces your value or standard. Your value is the equivalent of your purpose. Values are parameters of judgment. If I know the values or standards you keep, I can precisely determine your future. Acting without value is acting without purpose. Your value determines your contribution.

The value of purpose is to create leadership and make it more effective. All value of our being is hidden in our purpose. To create wealth and success, we must demonstrate and fully express our passion in the direction of our purpose. Purpose makes us lead our life by influencing the earth. Leadership is nothing more than influence. For leadership to serve its purpose, and be meaningful and fulfilling, it must bring value to the earth. When a leader is dedicated to a purpose, great things happen because he brings value to the table. His impact affects everybody positively.

What is the value of purpose? Purpose is central to

leadership. All virtues and skills of leadership are connected to purpose. There cannot be leadership without purpose. All leaders start with dreaming, they dream about their purpose, from their purpose, they create a vision, from the vision they move to create goals, and from goals they extract their reward. Leaders express their passion in everything they do.

The purpose of value always defined how a leader serves and contributes to the well-being of humanity. Purpose provides value for leadership to contribute to the cause of empowering humanity. The value of leadership is central to the contribution it brings to people who do not know the direction to better their lives. People naturally complain when there is a leadership vacuum or the perceived leader is leading without purpose. Leadership is value towards contribution. Look at every leader you ever knew, they derived their leadership from the contribution of empowering humanity. Henry Ford's purpose was to make cars for the people from the best possible materials at a reasonable price which is affordable to all men with average earnings. Andrew Carnegie's purpose was to make money for the first part of his life and invest it in contributing to empowering people for the other part of his life.

Purpose centered on value creates leadership for social change. Leadership based on purpose attributes its value on influence while leadership not driven by purpose attributes its existence on the accumulation of power that is used authoritatively to subjugate society to a standstill. While purposeful leadership promotes progress, purposeless leadership arrests progression and development. While purposeful leadership promotes change, purposeless leadership denies and resists change. It only changes from the status quo that offers development.

Purpose is the only valuable opportunity a leader uses in promoting change and influencing the cooperation of social efforts, time, and resources in making a pathway into the future of unlimited possibilities.

IX. ***Purpose determines focus***

Purpose determines focus. Purpose provides direction and the direction you are heading is a function of your focus. Everything you will ever be in life will be determined by your focus. What you are consistently focusing your life on has a tremendous impact on the quality and direction of your life. Since the value of purpose is in contributing to humanity, your purpose therefore must concern itself with the service it will give to humanity. Purpose rests on the principle of service. All-purpose have a strong element of service to deliver. What is your passion? Whom are you using it to serve? What difference will it make? Make it your magnificent obsession; put all your focus on the joy of fulfilling your purpose, for it will first bring you joy more than anything else.

X. ***Purpose measures your attitude***

Purpose measures your attitude. The quality of your life will come down to the quality of your contribution. The quality and value of your contribution to the marketplace will determine the size of your wealth. Do things with determination and commitment to a noble cause. Have a passion for excellence. Create values that are consistent with your purpose and vision. Such Values should be the standard of your attitude in pursuing and reflecting the purpose, vision, and goals that you truly seek.

Purpose gives meaning, fulfillment, and direction to your life; and your attitude molds the path toward that direction. Attitude is passion fully expressed. Attitude is the building block of life. Unless you work and build your attitude towards the direction of your purpose, you are heading nowhere to a meaningless future. Everything you do must significantly count toward achieving your purpose and the zeal with which you express your passion and commitment towards your purpose is a measurement of your attitude.

The strength of your attitude will determine the speed with which you advance toward the direction of your purpose. Unless you can see your purpose- the big picture of your life- it would not make sense to quicken your attitude to measure up towards fulfilling your purpose. The prize of life is in fulfilling your purpose and it is constantly measured by the strength or weakness of your attitude. Attitude determines the pattern through which we decide and act on everything concerning our life's purpose. The way we do anything is the way we do everything and this virtually determines the outcome of all we truly do, become, and have. Attitude is everything that will fix our fate.

XI. ***Purpose sustains your belief***

Purpose sustains your belief. Life is a journey of purpose, unless you believe in your purpose, you will not make the journey. You will not bring your passion to express your purpose even if you attempt to make the journey. Making life's journey is central to purpose. It is the only purpose that can sustain belief; this is because it is only in purpose you can find meaning, fulfillment, and direction for your life.

At every point in our life's journey, it is belief in our purpose that gives us the courage to contribute to humanity. Those living without purpose are the ones giving humanity its critical challenges. Leadership is lacking in human society today because those who find themselves in positions of authority lack the purpose of service and contribution. Leadership is connected with purpose and vision for humanity. Faith in your purpose is the foundation of belief. If you have not discovered your purpose, you can believe in anything. It is only with a purpose that we can find meaning in our existence.

It is with a purpose that the world was created and it is with a purpose that we exist at this particular time in it. Many of us go through life only seeking to get from life without thinking of our contribution and service to humanity. A life without service to humanity is ungodly and lacks purpose. Service to humanity is the worship of God. It is only when we know our purpose and expresses it in our passion with full commitment that we truly exist. Purpose precedes existence. Until we believe in our purpose, we do not yet exist.

Success is discovering and fulfilling your purpose; Success is who you are. Success happens to you when you are fulfilling your purpose and you are contributing to the betterment of humanity. Wealth is just a reward for doing so. You must learn to believe in yourself and your purpose. Whatever you truly believe will become your reality. Believe in your purpose and manifest it.

XII. ***Purpose guarantees success.***

Purpose guarantees success. Until you know your purpose, you can never succeed at it. your responsibility in life is to discover and fulfill your life purpose. Unless you know your purpose, you will never find your place in it. What happens to you if you do not know the destination of where you are going? How will you locate your route to your destination? We have shared in this work that your purpose is the big picture of your life and your vision is its destination. So without a purpose, there is no destination. Since the destination is located on purpose and you are existing without one; then where are you heading? If you do not know your destination, any road will lead you nowhere. Have you ever found yourself in a strange place and suddenly discovered you are lost?

Without a compass, you cannot get to where you are going. Your purpose is your compass. It determines the route to your destination- the big picture of your life. It is only when you have discovered your purpose, you have a clear vision of it and you are determined to walk through the path to the big picture, that success is guaranteed.

Success is attached to purpose. There cannot be a success without purpose, yet the majority of people go through life without a purpose. Less than 3% of people go through life with purpose; No wonder many people are not successful in life. For every purpose, there is always a plan. No one builds a house without a plan, yet the same person wants to build a life without a purpose and a plan. The ultimate key to wealth and success is having a clear visible purpose. Purpose always guarantees success.

XIII. ***Purpose produces rewards***

Purpose produces a reward. Everyone has a purpose but the significance of the purpose is to contribute to humanity. Though this is intended to make humanity better, the vendor of the purpose also receives a reward by the virtue of the value of his contribution. Every time you contribute, you are significantly compensated by the same action. It is a corresponding factor. As much as you contribute to humanity, you are increasingly compensated. He that watered shall also be watered. As a man sows, so he will reap. For every cause, there is an effect.

The law of attraction is bringing back your contribution in hundreds, thousands, and millions of folds. These are timeless universal principles that are unbroken. The reward of purpose is manifested in extreme wealth, great success, and most significant life fulfillment. For every one that contributes to humanity, an abundance of wealth is his reward; therefore, for every single purpose, there is extreme unlimited wealth, great success, and life's fulfillment.

XIV. ***Purpose releases freedom***

Purpose releases freedom. Every man is born with a purpose but most people go through life without getting fulfillment because they are dethatched from their purpose. They are constrained and misdirected by social pressures from external counter forces imposed from outside of them rather than from deep within. These social pressures derived from parents, guidance, religious, ethnic, and even educational system are counterforces that stand in the way of people's passion, and as a consequence people are turning away from their passion. Once people are disconnected from their passion, they lost contact and connection with their calling, voice, instruction, inclination, vocation, compass, the big picture, assignment, or purpose.

You become imprisoned in a new outer world and disconnected from the world within. Counterforces are put up against your passion and purpose because of the immediate fame and money it will allow you to get by temporarily. This is a dangerous path to tread as it will make you lose focus on your purpose and imprison you in a large outer world with no space to accommodate you and your passion.

Your passion is the key to unlocking your freedom. Until you fully express your passion through the lifestyle that you choose, you will never find meaning and fulfillment in your life. Your passion is always seeking avenues to fully express itself but until you focus your passion on your purpose, you won't get the satisfaction that comes from getting meaning and fulfillment. Passion is directed towards purpose to bring meaning and fulfillment to your life among other things.

Imagine that you suddenly found yourself in a strange big

house with only one firmly locked iron exit door and you have tried to open the door for more than a week but it seems there is nothing you can do to open the door to get out of your prison. All efforts to push the door through to the other side had only produced pain for you. After all the trials of strength, you now discover you have dissipated all the energy inside you to open the door but the door still shut you inside the house. You finally gave up and started sleeping, waiting, and wondering how you got here. Who are your captors? What are they likely to do to you? What is their purpose in keeping you inside this house as a prisoner? While you are wondering and wandering in an endless search for answers, you finally slept off on a mat inside one of the forty rooms of the empty house.

After a series of hours of deep sleep, you abruptly snapped into life from a dream. Six kilometers from where you are sleeping were coming from suspicious noise from your captors advancing towards your prison. With desperation to get out of the prison, you suddenly remember that you dreamt and saw a key under the mat you are now standing on. You instantly got the mat off your feet and behold a key was glaring at you. You picked the key and headed for the door and with one turn of the key at the lock, the door opened.

The daylight of the sun of opportunities greeted you with fresh air as you busted out into freedom. Once you were out you discovered no one was holding you captive but yourself. This is the story of many who are trapped inside life without a purpose and a passion to free them.

Passion and purpose are inseparable. Passion is the only key to freedom but purpose gives the reason, provides the motive, and acts as releasing force for the expression of your passion. For every purpose, there is always a passion. You are a prisoner in this life until you discover your purpose and express your passion. You are always standing on top of the key to your freedom but you have to discover the purpose for the key or your passion before you can use it. If you are not fulfilled, your life has no meaning and you are searching for a direction to seek your freedom from the pains of imprisonment, then you are desperately in need of a purpose. Once there is a purpose, there is always passion to release you to your freedom; freedom from servitude, hunger, and meaninglessness of this world.

XV. ***Purpose answers your life's unending questions***

and settles its worries.

Purpose answers your life's unending questions and settles its worries. An unexamined life is not worth living. Anytime you examine a tired, boring, and unexciting life, you are going to see a life without purpose, dissipated passion, a series of unending questions, and a worried mind. The analogy of our previous story best illustrates a typical life situation. Most people only seat to ponder when they are overwhelmed with life's problems and worries resulting from the meaninglessness of their lives. What many fail to understand is that the questions they later ask themselves are in essence the same questions they ought to have first asked before the problems.

Questions are the real guide to avoiding life worries. It is a path to finding and discovering one's purpose. Every great discovery begins by asking the right questions. Until you ask the right question, the truth about your purpose is hidden from you. If you truly seek greatness, then ask the greatest question. What is the meaning of my life, what is my purpose, why am I here, and what is my contribution? What can I give in exchange for my life? And what is my passion?

The quality of your life is significantly determined by the

nature of the question you ask yourself. When you ask the right question, your mind search for the answer you seek in the universe. Ask empowering questions- they bring you life's meaning, fulfillment, extreme wealth, and great success. Every question has a positive answer. Every question is a cause; the answer is an effect.

The question you habitually and consistently ask yourself determines everything about your life. Question is seeking answers to problems or worries. It is different from complaining.

Question determines your focus. What are you asking about your purpose, your finance, your health, your family, your friends, your business, your community, or humanity? The world is waiting for you to discover your purpose and bring into fulfillment your contribution. Ask the right questions, to get focused on your purpose.

XVI. ***Purpose is your life's Ultimate Power.***

Purpose is your life's ultimate power; everything in your life is centered on it. Passion is the key to unleashing or releasing it to you. Passion is an element of power and purpose is the power to bring into fulfillment your contribution. The only significance that rationalizes your existence is your purpose and its contribution to humanity. At last, everything counts and points in the direction of your purpose. Purpose provides you with the ultimate power to deliver your contribution. Your purpose is a function of necessity that humanity cannot ignore. No man can function outside of his purpose and gain meaning and fulfillment. The power necessary to go through life with impacting your world is only found in purpose.

The purpose of your existence, therefore, is to enrich humanity through your contribution and it only requires purpose to fulfill it. Without the power released by your purpose, you are not making the journey but only wandering. Since purpose implies making the journey of life to the big picture or destiny, when there is no purpose, there is no destination, and energy utilized in the pursuit of purposelessness is wasted and will end in disaster. Many lives have gone in history with no impact because those who carry them went without purpose and pitifully without power.

The Power of Purpose is your magic to exploring the unlimited possibilities of the universe and its underlining current connection to you. Your purpose is like a switch attached to the universe's current. It is only waiting for you to switch it on to experience the freedom and power of finding your passion and fully expressing it; focus, take action on your passion and master it to greatness; guard against negative emotional and social programming; live each day with integrity, discipline and commitment to your assignment, discover who you are and get fulfillment knowing what your contribution is and to who and become everything you will ultimately want to be, do and have. The power of your purpose is inexhaustible. You only need to explore it for your contribution and humanity enrichment.

XVII. **Purpose Resonate Love.**

Nothing will work in your life if you disconnect from your purpose and passion. Purpose resonates with love and vibrates it throughout your life's work in bringing you fulfillment. Everything done for your purpose is in exchange for your life and is only the passion that you fully express that counts. What is the purpose when it fails to connect to your passion? What then is passion if there is no love in your assignment? If your work is boring and eating you up, then you are in the wrong vocation.

Time is an illusion of your passion. When you remember the tickling of time in your work, you are operating outside your passion. Passion ultimately is the love of your work and not the work of your pay. When your life vocation or career fails to bring you joy, love, and happiness of the spirit, then you are operating and working in a lost world. A world so big but empty, a world so rich but lacks wealth, a world so religious but without morality, conscience, and principle, a world with fast-moving planes but without direction and destination.

Only the love of your passion will make the difference and give meaning to your life's exchange. Purpose only resonates with love when the three secrets of time and its four opportunities are revealed to you. To live life to its fullest, you must discover and recover your purpose.

Chapter Three

DETERMINATION

Determination is a magnificent key to success that resonates with faith in the purpose of life. It births the desire to craft the vision that sees the destination of your purpose, fuels your passion, initials a clear, specific goal that is in tandem with the big picture, spurs the zeal to initiate the plan of action and take the required steps and efforts necessary to get the fulfillment that success brings.

No one can succeed without the determination to get to the end of the picture and destination of purpose. It does not matter how far you go in life. What matters most is having the determination and courage to go through a journey with the persistence of hope to get the prize and reward of success.

The route to success may have unexpected and shocking outcomes and challenges that may threaten the actualization of achieving a purpose. There are twisty and mysterious obstacles that will stand against the will to succeed in reaching the end. If success was easy, everybody would have been successful. Success comes with responsibility, hard work, persistence, and courage to go through a planned course of action that is unclear but constantly requires refinement and adjustment to navigate the course to the end of the vision's big picture.

Determination rest on the belief that purpose is the singular objective of life that provides the zeal to focus on well-crafted goals and the plan of actions attached to them. Determination provides the energy of sustainability that drives the passion to bring to fulfillment the realization of purpose. Determination promotes the quest to connect purpose to an aligned passion and transform passion into dedicated sets of skill that strengthens the capabilities to function adequately. It is the quality of functionality that defines the performance of tasks targeted at the fulfillment of purpose.

Determination is inward driven and requires a positive

conviction and affirmation to go through to the end of the journey. This means determination is self-driven or self-determinate based on the resolve to get satisfaction and the fulfillment is brings. It strengthens the unwavering resolve to make critical choices and the resilient of power to make decisions that truly keep you in control of your life.

Your circle of influence and the means to navigate life is a function of determination. Determination is manifested in the combined value of respect, contribution, service, meaning, achievement, advancement, commitment, responsibility, result-oriented and performance-driven choices that increase control, happier life, mattering, relationship with the community, and personal fulfillment.

Determination is the secured active will that inspires and motivates people to dream bigger than self and beyond the present. It is the will to overcome failure and the desire to add meaning to the force of persistence that secures defined results and expectations. Ella Wheeler Wilcox noted that there is no chance, no destiny, no fate, that can hinder or control the firm resolve of a determined soul.

Chapter Four

MONEY

Money in itself is an idea of expressing value and a scares commodity that dignifies efforts or results. It is the most sought-after commodity in the universe yet is not wealth. Money is a universal commodity and therefore reflects a universal equivalent with the exchange value for all other commodities. It is only through it that all other commodities can be universally and equivalently measured.

Money is the value worth of a commodity. So, the value of a commodity is converted, exchanged, stored, or measured in money. The usefulness of a commodity, therefore, determines its exchange value; therefore, a commodity is a thing that possesses properties that promise to satisfy human wants or needs. Every commodity must therefore be useful or valuable to attract money that multiplies systematically into wealth.

Kevon Five Laws of Money

The kevon's five laws of money explain the nature and character of money; if you want plenty of money flowing into your life you must apply the eternal principle that they demonstrate. They are given to you as a bonus, keep these laws seriously and you will never be bankrupt in your life. This is a guaranteed promise.

Many money = There are many, plenty, abundant, and unlimited money circulating in the universe and connecting to your life. It is hidden in your purpose. Find your purpose and you are already holding all the money of your life in your hand. This is not a mere motivational or inspirational talk/speech to make you get excited. If you find your purpose, you will amass money in your life. I have said repeatedly to you before now that your purpose is your exchange. What are you exchanging your life for? Answering this singular question is the inescapable answer to attract money and wealth in your possession/life.

Your purpose is your life bank account, why are you not withdrawing from it? Your purpose is not filled with your life's wealth if you are consistently broke. What is happening to you? When I see a consistently broke man, I see a man that has not found his purpose. If you consider the subject of purpose weird and difficult to comprehend, how about your passion? Your passion is the other equation of your fulfillment. They both lead you to the same destination- your destiny. You can start living your purpose by feeding your passion.

What are you waiting for? Your purpose or your passion leads you to the abundant life that you have been called to live. The creator never intended for you to live miserably. Everybody was created with a purpose and passion to express their wealth. No man is ever poor except he permits it. If you do the things you love and are good at it; plenty of money will rush into your purse.

Opportunity and Optimism = Money only follows problems. Problems are opportunities. Problem solvers regularly attract opportunities and money to themselves. Optimists are people who only see opportunities in front of them. Put an obstacle in front of an optimist, he will convert it into an opportunity. Your purpose creates opportunities and your passion explores them. Opportunities are limitless; you can continuously create them with your mind. The power of your mind is manifested in visualization (imagine great things and explore opportunities you can create with your mind) and verbalization (articulation of positive words).

Continually used them to create opportunities and enrich yourself. These are powerful forces you can use to create your life. You that you are a god in disguise. So start creating your life with your purpose.

Have you heard about the ant philosophy? The ants are a wonderful creature, so tiny, so small yet they are the wisest of all creatures. They keep their food in the summer and have plenty of stored harvest in the winter. They are never hungry. Put a blockage in the front of an ant, he will immediately climb it with vigour and optimism. The ant is a wonderful organism that is so organized. Ants move in large numbers; they form an army to do a single task. Keep a loaf of bread in a secret place, they will find it and break it into smaller units without tools and before you know it, they will transport its piecemeal to their destination. The ant is so full of purpose and passion that you cannot stop it. If you prevent the ant from getting through to a path a thousand times, it must find a way.

No matter where you keep sugar, ants will always find it. Ants are naturally attracted to sugar. Ants are optimists; they never give up, no matter what. Even if you block access to a million paths to their destination, they will dig a tunnel there. They are always persistent, determined, and passionate about their purpose. Develop the persistence, determination, and passionate capacity of the ant and you will always have plenty of money in your possession.

Neutrality = Money is neutral. It does not discriminate against people. It does not respect class, religion, age, location, ethnicity, culture, race, or sex. If you obey the laws of money by doing the needful, it will come to meet you in abundance. Money follows good and exciting ideas. If you want money, attract it to your life. Money is a very shy object, if you want plenty of it; attract it to yourself by feeding your passion and living your purpose.

You are a living magnet; the more valuable you are, the more money you will attract into your life. Continuously seek to multiply your value a hundredfold and beyond on compounding interest. Money is neutral; it gladly goes to those who are valuable no matter who they are, where they live, and what they do.

Entrepreneur's Servant = Money is the entrepreneur's servant and labourers-employees' master. Entrepreneurs are masters in the game of money. They are excellent in anything they do and most importantly they do it skillfully and passionately. Entrepreneurs turn their passion and skills into a business. They first contribute to humanity through their business and money naturally follows. They enjoy making money. They produce values in limitless quantities. They create and build a business and allow their business to print money while they sleep. Entrepreneurs do not work in their business or work for others; they create a business that takes care of itself. They only nurture and give it direction. They are creative, resourceful, thoughtful, and imaginative; they spend less than they earn and reinvest a huge part of their profit. Profits are better than wages.

Entrepreneurs know their purpose and they are focused on the goals necessary to achieve their purpose. They are 100% responsible for the direction of their business. They always make a difference and anything they touch turns into gold-money. They improve and add value to anything that concerns them. They are purpose-driven and visionary; they create change for society and ultimately build wealth and legacy from it.

Yield time, skills, passion, and effort for Entrepreneur's business.

Employees sell or exchange their time, skills, passion, and efforts for Entrepreneur's profit. Anyone who sells his passion, effort, and skills for a fixed income is undermining the law of the averages. You are averagely rewarded according to the number of effort and value you produce. When you work in another man's business, your chances of earning your owing money are slim. This means he forecloses the chances of exploring his life opportunity for another man's advantage. All he gets is a pay cheque equivalent to the size of his fear. It is unbelievable to see people whose life is completely budgeted on serving another man's profit in exchange for their wages, and thereafter ignoring their purpose.

Let me fix your mind from the right perspective. Do you know that employers only hire people who are valuable to their business? The reason for this is that the employer of your service is hiring your whole time and being for a fee? They expect to extract your genius and put it to work for their benefit. Do you know no employer will ever pay you the worth or equivalent of your value in comparison with the time you put in every month? If you figure it out, you are selling yourself too cheap only because of fear.

Don't get me wrong that working in another business as an employee is all wrong. It is only justifiable if you are doing it to get experience and mentorship for the growth of your own proposed business or significantly to raise initial capital to start your own business. I will accept that as a consideration of the obvious if the purpose of your work is for the projection of a defined purpose.

Statistics don't favour those who eke out all their life working for another man's profit. Do you know why? Jim Rohn's answer will aid you to understand properly that profits are better than wages, wages will make you a living but profit will make you a fortune. If you want to make a living then you can remain in employment till your retirement and go hungry, broke, and die miserable regretting not fixing things earlier in life. I guess the regret always comes when it's too late in life to do anything, especially making the needful change when it is necessary.

Statistics show that 95% of employees retired broke and about half of this percentage goes homeless at retirement. It is just funny to see that it is only 5% of employees can get rich at retirement age. I wonder if the probability will favour you among this lucky 5%. The bottom line here is that if you work in a business, whether you own it, you are only selling your time and I know it will be a slight chance for you to get rich under such an arrangement.

A final word on the law of money; money is an idea and its creation starts in the mind, attracts the right idea, manifests it and an abundance of opportunities and money will continuously flow into your life.

Chapter Five

TIME AND OPPORTUNITIES

Opportunities are out there waiting for only the person who is attracted to them. Opportunities exist in time; one man gets up early to seek opportunities and another man sleeps in bed waiting for opportunities to wake him up. The former encounters opportunities and converts them into wealth, the latter sobs in poverty because opportunities are wanderers, you can only encounter them when you walk their path.

Everything about creating wealth revolves around time. One principal thing that differentiates the engagement of any of the four vehicles of the wealth creation manifest is your use of time- the universal currency. How you use your time will ultimately decide what vehicle you have chosen to board on the wealth creation manifest. Remember that time is a currency and how you use your passion concerning time can affect the flow of money into your life.

There are three times of your life (the trinity of time) and four opportunities you can derive from it. The three times of your life are the PAST, the PRESENT, and the FUTURE. The four opportunities are located in three of the times mentioned.

The opportunity of your PAST is the experience you create from it. Most of your success and failure in wealth creation manifest are generated from your experience of the past. Most people advise that you put your past behind you and walk in the present and future. This is not a wise decision to make. You can fail forward. You can learn something from those failures of the past and explore their weakness and learn not to do so again. The experience they say is the best teacher.

Also, you need the experience of your past to give you the required confidence to move on. The experience of your failures and your success shapes your programming for the present and in the future. You must preserve the experience of the past and learn how to use it to your advantage in shaping your wealth creation experience. Many people who lack experience are paying to earn it in the school of life in their present life.

Experience creates mentors in every endevours of life. Most of our present success comes from the challenges of our past experiences. Experience is the only opportunity we bring from our past into our present and future. How we use these experiences in the present and the future, will ultimately make the difference in our lives and determine the size of our success.

Our experience of the past is the only leverage we have above others in the present and in the future to come. The past is not completely gone; we carry the experience of it with us to model the present and the future. We all cannot live in the same world in our present because of the diversity of our rich deep past experiences. The experience of the past has its passion that is relevant in shaping, making, and revolutionizing who we become in the present and in the future to come.

The PRESENT is the biggest opportunity we will ever have. It is the future of yesterday and represents the completion of our past expectations. If we know our purpose, express our passion, see the vision and design the road map of yesterday, it will lead us to the future of yesterday.

Today is a miracle; it is the reality of yesterday's expectation. We either designed it consciously or by default. It is never an accident. The present is our making. A large part of the present happened because of our yesterday's practice that becomes today's consequence or outcome. We have the opportunity to shape today's practice or experiment better and bigger than in the past. We can continue the practice of yesterday's experience if the outcome is desirable and experiment if the change is required to gain a new expectation.

Every experience of yesterday can be adjusted today to give a more meaningful impact. It is called learning from the past and putting it into practice for today's benefits. Everything that comes to us today that is not in our past, we attract through education and experiments. Today's present opportunities are greater and bigger than yesterday's past. The present opportunities are therefore what we learn through education and what we experiment with through trying out what we seek to be the truth we desire. In reality, the opportunities of the present are education and experiments.

Our past brought us to today. If we are inadequate with today, then our experience is not enough to give us the life we dreamt of. If the past is inadequate, then we have the responsibility to contribute something meaning to improve the mistake of the past or provide something different. If the past did not get us to where we want to go, we have to find another route to where we ought to be. Most of us know our expectations; we can feel them deep inside us.

The destination is given to us deep inside of us from our purpose. Whatever the difference is in our life, we can take responsibility and make a great change with another paradigm that we have not previously considered. If our experience of the past is inadequate, our experiment with the present can compensate for it. On the other side, we are too afraid to take the part we never considered making can be experimented with today to compensate for yesterday's failures.

By experimenting, we are sincerely recreating the world we truly desire. No part of the world was created once; all we see today are products of experimentation. Our today's experiment will be yesterday's experience in the future. It is the experiment that is significantly constant. Our individuality is buried in the experiments of the present that we boldly take. This is where passion thrives. Our passion expresses our purpose and reflects it.

From our purpose, our passion continuously brings us insights and pictures of our purpose and the difference we are intended to create. Our genius is the expression and fulfillment of our purpose. The experiment is constantly and patiently staying in tune with your passion to bring about the fulfillment of your purpose. Thomas Edison, Steve Jobs, Warren Buffet, and countless others have seen success through their experiments. No one handed a manual of success to them; they expressed their passion by experimenting with insights revealed to them from their vision. You too can experiment with your passion in the fulfillment of your purpose.

No one can claim to know it all. Our experiment involves trials and errors in gaining ways of expressing passion. We learn from our mistakes and repeatedly improve on them. Continuous improvement is generated from the application of organized knowledge through experimentation. There is a greater passage of our passion into wealth today for us if we lead the world from our experiments. Experimental knowledge essentially produces a unique body of cause-and-effect relationships concerning the goal. If the cause is then discovered in this process, a fact is acquired and replicated as future experience. A breakthrough in business and other aspects of life are derived from experimentation.

We may not be able to capture every part of the globe without the help of others. Much of what we know today, significantly comes from others, even our programming. Our education comes from the success and failures of people's experiences but not our own. We already have ours but we must deliberately and continuously search for more knowledge and understanding about how other people's past can help change and shape our present.

If you want to know yourself, you can look at other people's past experiences and you will see the expression of passion you have not acquired. Every person who succeeds in the expression of your desire knows something you are ignorant of in the past. The human experience is so diverse and deep-seated that you cannot completely live them but you can share their experience through education.

Education becomes the modeling of the human

consciousness to reflect the aspect of the cosmos that is hidden or not visible to you in the past. Everything experienced by a large number of people in priceless times past can be learned through codifying them into the principle of tablets for easy access.

Education has been the best expression of the human experience from the foundation of the world shared among enlightened minds. If you open your mind, the benefits from these experiences can be given to you without sharing the pain exploited to get them. Education takes peoples' past pains and converts them into today's pleasures. The accumulation of today's civilization is the expression of yesterday's experiences open to us through learning. The painful case is that people are reluctant to learn about the magnificent path to success.

The size of today's opportunities comes from our education of people's past experiences codified into working principles and our experiment of what is missing to fill the world. The result of our experiments has a larger chunk in shaping the world by its contribution and the wealth it brings to us. Our experiment invariably shapes other people's education.

The opportunities of today simply impress on our ability to

borrow from others' experiences of the past and add to our experience and experiment of today. Thus making today's opportunities greater than yesterday's. In the past, we are unaware of these experiences and cannot utilize them because they are still been processed- experimented with where we cannot reach them.

The FUTURE is tomorrow and ahead of us but we can live in it with our imagination. Every one of the opportunities we exploit today was first created in our past imagination. Imagination is creating the future today. If we can create the future today, then we are invariably living in it today. We are thus borrowing the future we want to live in and hope to manifest it when the time comes.

The work of creation happens through the power of imagination. If you can imagine anything by strongly concentrating your mind to draw a clear picture of the future you desire, you are creating reality in advance. We first live in the world of imagination before we get there. This is the strongest of all the opportunities because there is no limitation in its creation.

Nothing can prevent imagination. All universal laws are adequately suspended in imagination. Everything obeys and recognizes the power of imagination. The universe adequately responds to it. Most people limit their mind and power of imagination to the limit of their experience and the limits of their education. To some extent, little of our experiment is shaped by logic with no imagination. Imagination thus is future thinking that we can advance to live in today and take advantage of. Imagination is the only tool with which you can create your goal or road map that will drive you to the future from where you are. Very few people dwell in this future realm and take significant opportunities arising from it.

All the times and the opportunities therein are an expression of your passion that can be manifested to create extreme wealth today. If you know what you want, you can get it today by how you use your time and the ceaseless opportunities buried in time. Wealth is therefore time in passion or passion expressed in time.

Expressing your passion in time will require one of the four vehicles of wealth creation manifest. The four vehicles to create wealth are WORK, INVEST, REAL ESTATE, and BUSINESS.

Work

Wealth is passion expressed in time. Work is principally selling your time to express your passion for the benefit of another man's pleasure. You are only acquired as an asset to work in exchange for money. The size of the money you get in exchange for the time you are selling is considered your self-worth. Nobody will pay you the equivalent of your true self-worth. Whenever you are recruited to work in an enterprise, the aim of that enterprise is principally to make a profit. It does so by paying you less of your true self-worth to make an adequate profit to stay in business and to keep you in employment. Why is this so? Because you never believed in yourself and entrepreneurs know this fact and they are exploiting it for their benefit.

If you are not valuable, no entrepreneur or business will hire you. Businesses do not hire tramps, if they discover a tramp in their business, he gets the boot without delay. Businesses only hire smart and valuable people who can create more value for them. The truth of the matter is that smart enterprises hire your passion more than they hire your personality. The time you are selling is fixed but the value you generate in exchange for the time must be positively immeasurable to keep you in employment.

The greatest value to an employee is not the value he produces but the security he gets from the job that pays for his exchange value. When you work in another man's enterprise, you are selling your time and passion in exchange for money. You gain security but you are losing your exchange and invariably your purpose. Your true exchange is your purpose and not money. Money is a supply of wealth. Money is a means to getting wealth. Your wealth is located in your purpose and money cannot even qualify for your exchange. Reevaluate your goal and see if your work is giving you meaning and fulfillment. Deep down inside you, you know you are not in control of what you are doing in your work. The purpose is about taking control of your life.

The value exchange equivalent of your time and pay is on a ratio of 90:10. This means you are only paid a maximum of 10% of the value you produce. Most profession earns between 5% to 10% value they create on a commission. You can never be wealthy this way because what you produce far exceeds the reward you get in return for the passion you express. How valuable you are to your employer will decide the size of your pay. To get more pay, become more valuable. You must learn to do what only a few people are capable of doing. You must show your difference to get more value. The value of your pay rises higher when you do what only a few people can do. Your passion or skill must be relatively scarce and valuable to earn more. To earn more pay, you must become more valuable by doing what is difficult for many people to do.

The unfortunate story of the majority of workers is that they are engaged in jobs that people do not want to do. In a sense, these are regular jobs that do not require many skills to do. The abundance of the skill required to do such jobs makes them low valued or inexpensive in their earnings.

You really cannot become wealthy selling your time in making more of your value reaped off you. What you get in exchange for the value you donate is disproportionately in your favour. Over time you seem to donate a larger portion of your value to your employer and you always end up broke. Your life meaning and your existence tends to strongly depend on the security of continually holding on to your job. The danger of continuing to hold on to the job is that it makes you always vulnerable to external control and manipulation. When you lack personal control of your life direction, you lose your purpose, your contribution, meaning, and fulfillment.

The value you produce in a job is strongly located in the time and money that is exchanged for it. If you stop working, you will end up broke and financially insecure. The money will stop flowing. There is therefore no guarantee of your continued existence in the job. Most jobs leave you with nothing before the next pay cheque and you are obliged to continue producing value to enrich your employer while you are getting broke and unfulfilled.

This condition never allows you of using your experience, your present education and experiment, and your future imagination for your financial independence to enrich yourself. This is the worst you can ever be in life; to be continuously hooked to a state of dependency, where you work in another man's purpose and tend to live outside of your purpose without meaning and fulfillment.

Working life is a lesser life with no autonomy to act on your purpose because your time to do that is already sold. It is only a tiny fraction of the working people that ever get wealthy and escape the broke trap, just less than 5% who are extremely valuable and are earning a greater chunk of their value but again this is rare. They are usually placed on the top of the hierarchy of the work organization or they are among the best 10% in their profession.

They get there with a lot of wasted energy and do not stay there long before retirement. The whole idea of clinching a job is accepting you are with no purpose and you are ready to take anything life offers you because it does not matter how you end up. I call this living a self-defeat life. Consider this: if you only earn maximally 10% of your value and give out 90% of it, when are you going to get wealthy and be financially independent? This is enslaving yourself and it will only help you stay stuck in your job. So get out of the job as soon as you can. My only advice to you before leaving the job, get the relevant skills of replicating the work structure and use it for your benefit. You can only be wealthy when you control the mechanism that produces the value you earn. Do it for yourself than getting it from another person.

If you must work, work to gain experience from a mentor in a business or organization that can expand the horizon of your passion. You can become of better value by spending your time acquiring experience and transforming your passion.

NEVER STAY IN A WORK ORGANIZATION

BEYOND COPYING THE SYSTEM THAT IS PAYING YOU AND DO NOT FORGET TO STOCK SOME SAVINGS ON YOUR WAY OUT- never leave empty. This should be your only mission to work, your time is your currency, and use it for yourself. Your primary concern before you leave the job is to work to learn. Let it be your apprenticeship phase on your way to acquiring mastery of your passion.

Invest.

You can eat your cake and have it too but you have to first lend it out on interest. Investment is letting your money work for you while you do something else but the control of your money is still subject to an external influence other than you. If it is slavery to work for money, then you can turn the table around and let your money work for you instead. Isn't this amazing- You should make your money work in your place.

If you give your money to another person to work for you instead of you doing the work, you will get paid for your money even bigger than you can work. The rich do this every time. They put their treasure where they want it to multiply. They watch their money multiply with time. Your money can work round the clock the way you cannot. Money is always an obedient servant if you know how to direct it. Investment is part owner of an enterprise and sharing out in the profit of it. Your money only takes a risk by working where is it invested.

When you work, you invest your passion and time for money but when you invest your money, you are risking the money you are investing. Risk varies inversely with knowledge. The size of your knowledge will vary with the risk you take with your money. If you invest in an opportunity that you do not have adequate knowledge of and cannot determine the level of uncertainty that will arise, your risk is high. If your risk is high, there are chances you will lose all your money or a certain part of it.

If you invest in any enterprise, you are buying some stock, shares, equities, or part of the business, you are putting your money into an investment. Since the money is going to be managed by someone else and not you, you must be careful to know everything that is required before putting your money to work there. Most investments are scams, the moment your money gets in, you are on the wrong flight heading to no destination. You must therefore only invest in a business that you have adequate knowledge of and the management of a business with high integrity and value.

Ask a lot of questions to be 100% certain. Never take the owner's words hook line and sinker, listen completely, and read between lines, there is always something missing. Smell the rat if it is in there. Never invest with your emotion, invest wisely with the size of your knowledge of the business you are comfortable with. Always know the numbers before you invest. Check the history of the business and do a critical survey before you let go of your money into an investment and never allow the beneficiary to advise you. Limit your investment decision only to the products you know very well and be sure to project into the future.

Investing in stock is very volatile, and adequate knowledge of fundamentals is necessary to be top of the game. Good knowledge of the stock market is profitable for the few who understand it. The stock market is highly fluctuating and inconsistent with regular up and down turns; it will always encounter crises and uncertainty. Predicting the period or year of down turn or up turn is very difficult. So investing in the short run is highly risky. The safest rule for investors in the stock market is to invest only for the long term. Adopt a buy-and-hold strategy only for the long term. There are usually fluctuations that make predictions unrealistic. Stock market predictions are usually 60% wrong. Stock holding is therefore a long-term investment. Stock returns are safely 4.5% on average and about 12% generally over the long term because of inevitable fluctuations that will drag your profit down.

Stock market crises are deep-seated and painful for short-term investors but cautionary for long-term investors with no harm- just the lessons. Stock market crises are inevitable and happen an average of 2 to 3 times every decade. The ultimate rule of investing in the stock market is not ever attempting to time the market performance, it is the riskiest mistake an investor will ever make, long term patience is the winner in the game. Do not ever sow with the crowd; stock investment is not a popularity contest.

Be smart to know what you are buying and who is managing it. Make sure it's entirely a simple product and it can be managed even by a dummy. Become a complete economy psychologist, only buy the stock when the market is depressed and sell when the boom is with the crowd, something terrible is about to happen. The stock market is profitable when it is cool and calm but is falling deep when there is excitement and noise everywhere about the value of a stock.

Stock investment is primarily a blind journey, it is risky for rush investors but a happy ride for slow travelers, slow and steady wins the race. It is a marathon; don't get on track with a spring attitude. It takes long years of investment to be profitable. Just simply invest 10% of your soft fund in a few stocks and sleep over the years and allow your money to grow. Sleep means forgetting your money there and pretending it does not exist. I guess your patience will reward you.

Real Estate

Real estate is the soul of wealth. It is where the souls of investors sleep. Real estate is a basic necessity for the human condition, a need we must continue to have as the human population increases and the material condition of man improves. It is now fashionable to live in mansions. No time ever more than now is real estate becoming the soul of business. Every human being stays in a house, their businesses and offices are run from buildings, buildings serve as recreations, hotels, schools, churches, and countless other accommodations. With civilization and urbanization, the real estate business is ever-expanding.

Real estate represents the title of converting money into wealth. It is an asset-building machine that retains the value of an investment. It is a smart investment portfolio for the wealthy. You can hardly point to a wealthy person who is not holding a sizeable portion of real estate. Most businesses' greatest assets are the properties that the business possesses. Why? Real estate hardly fluctuates; the truth is that its value increases by 50-100% per annual. Smart people invest their money in real estate because of its higher margin of profit over shares and it is an easily resalable value asset. You hardly resale real estate for less than a 50% return on investment; it is a winner's game.

You can acquire real estate gradually on a cheap funding plan by buying land and erecting a building on it at your pace. If your plan is to resale it, you can create a sizeable profit of more than 300% of your total investment. The use of real estate is unlimited and its earnings are immeasurable if you rent or lease it over time.

Real estate is an easy vehicle for raising funds for business. It is trustable collateral since its value is ever-increasing.

Investment in real estate requires innovation and patience but it is usually a huge investment for starters. Much it is investors' heaven in the time of crisis.

Real estate provides the best protection for investors in all circumstances. It is usually a man's shield when eventuality happens. A title to a real estate confirms your residential status and citizenry of a state. It is the best legal and business instrument you will ever rely on if you want to stay wealthy. It is usually the first count of wealth. Never stay without one. It is your best bet in overcoming vulnerability in life and business. Real estate is usually considered the last asset to build by everyone because it requires time and complexity of effort to own. However, it represents your freedom in a world of uncertainties.

Everything you can think of comes from land. Every mineral resource and food you eat comes from land. Adam was created out of it and it is a symbol of wealth God handed to Adam and not money, money is man's creation.

If you want to invest in real estate, you should buy properties in areas where development is moving in advance for at least five years. This is where vision counts in business. You should be able to forecast where development and people are heading in the next five years. Get there before they do and invest by adding value to the place before development sets in. if you buy in advance of development, you are going to buy with a profit margin of over 5000% and beyond; this is because people are attracted to development and jobs.

People want to stay close to their jobs, and social and public facilities. If you anticipate where these things are going to be built in advance, then start investing in them now. Buying property in strategic places though would require a large investment the premium is very high compared to the cost of investment. If you want to increase your leverage and opportunity to make real and substantial gains, you must add value to properties to attract higher rent, lease or sales.

Business

Business is the central activity of man's passion. Your business must reside in your passion if you want to create extreme wealth. Among the four vehicles of wealth, business is the ultimate and fastest way to create wealth. Business is also the only way to create extreme or massive wealth with lesser effort and time. A real business is a system of creating wealth. A system is a machine that runs on its own or operates on autopilot without effort and time. Business is a no-limit time machine. It reproduces endlessly.

A business is a system of organization of resources that produces value on an independent basis or with no interference from its owner. If you go to your business every day, then you are not in business but work in your business or are self-employed. You are simply a self-employed who hires himself to get out of unemployment.

A business runs itself independently of its owner and continuously recreates itself by reproducing values for profit. A business is an autonomous value machine. The only time an entrepreneur spends in its business is setting it up and occasionally visiting (vetting) it. This is building the wealth machine.

Follow God's Business Model

Business is a system, the system is order defined by purpose, the purpose is service, service is contribution and contribution is the fulfillment of necessity, necessity creates needs and business exists to satisfy these needs. Businesses must strive to respond to the service of necessity; they must devise a system of responding to the necessity which is the cause of human needs, well-being, and the manifestation of order.

All business arises from passion and any business which fails to observe the law of passion will vanish and be forgotten. Passion is the vehicle and energy of business and purpose. Every passion has its business and business is the wise expression of passion.

The system creates order in your business and order is a function of independence and noninterference. No organization, business, state, or society can function without a system. The system is self-autonomous. System and order are synonymous. Anywhere you see order; there is a system behind it. God's only passion or obsession is order. If the business is order and order is God's only obsession or passion, then God is the originator of business. It means God created a system to take care of HIS business and that is why the order is HIS obsession or passion.

Here is the proof: the universe is a giant system, and the solar system is another example. To narrow it to humanity and business, God's business is creation, and man's business is maintenance. God provides Leadership and Man manages God's enterprise. In Genesis chapter 1 God created everything including heaven and earth, light, and all creatures and plants between days 1 and 5 of creation. He qualified his creation to be good before he created and made man on day 6.

In Genesis 2:8, God put Adam in the Garden of Eden. Why put a man in a Garden? Two answers arise from this investigation. The first reason is that the Garden is God's creation (business) and it reflects a symbol of God's passion. A Garden is an orderly arrangement of plants in rows according to their species or kind. God put Adam in the Garden to show Adam his business, and the nature of the organized method of doing his work. This exemplary gesture demonstrated God's leadership to man. Adam, this is how you must organize the events, tasks, and activities of my business.

In Genesis 2:15, the second reason was given. God put Adam in the Garden of Eden to dress it and keep it. Man duties were specified in the business- to dress and keep the business- in order word, manage the business as I have shown you. Run the business on your own.

In Genesis 2: 16 and 17 God gave commandments, instructions, or charges of what not to do in the business.

In Genesis 2: 19, 'God gave Adam autonomy'41- freedom to execute his work. In Genesis 2: 19 and 20, Man started executing his responsibilities and God watched him perform his duties. In Genesis 2: 22, ‘God assisted Adam –Eve- is in the business to help Adam in the performance of his work. From here God left the business under Adam’s care.

In Genesis 3:8, God visited the business. In Genesis 3:9 God enquired about the business from Adam.

Why did God leave the business completely under Adam’s care?

God already created a system that guarantees the hands he deployed can take care of the business. With this system, the business takes care of itself without God’s effort and presence regulating the work to be done. The system once created, becomes an autopilot machine.

Once the Garden- business was created and Adam was instructed to dress and keep it with the assistance of Eve, a system was created as a structure to function in keeping and dressing the garden; God did not work in the Garden-business with them, he only visited and enquired. Once the business was created, God gave them autonomy to run the business without interference.

If you want to be successful in business, you must replicate

God's system. You can become godlike, 'God created man in his image and likeness46 (Genesis 1:26) and remember he showed Adam the Garden - Orchard business- this is mentorship. You can create a business with a system put in place that relieves you of your personal effort and time to run it.

James Allen in his book, Eight Pillars of Prosperity written as far back as 1911 (more than a century ago) said that every large business has its system which renders its vast machinery workable, enabling it to run like a well-balanced and oiled machine. James Allen confirmed this with the following story:

A remarkable businessman, a friend of mine, once told me that he could leave his huge business for twelve months, and it would run on without a hitch till his return; and he does occasionally leave it for several months while traveling and on his return (visit), every man, boy, and girl; every tool, book, and machine; every detail down to the smallest, is in his place doing its work as when he left; and no difficulty, no confusion has arisen.

Why Create Business With A System

A business with a system gives you leverage. The system

gives you the leverage of time to be completely free to multiply your time for unlimited opportunities. Time is fixed and cannot be altered but with a system, you can leverage time by multiplying it endlessly. All you have to do is delegate your business to a system that multiplies your time to accomplish what you will not have the chance to do while you are engaged in other activities. You can create multiple businesses with systems and benefit from all of them without your efforts. You can sleep (be away from the business) and earn residual income from multiple streams.

With the power of leverage, your system works for you while you sleep, doing nothing but claiming residual income and extreme wealth. This is what the rich do, the secret of their wealth is derived from business with a system that leverages time and earns residual income and extreme wealth.

You can only become wealthy if you become invisible in your business and earn from the leverage of time by doing many things at the same time. All the benefit comes back to

Residual Income.

The system allows your wealth to grow without restrictions. The system is created by putting the whole elements of your business into comprehensive utilities that are strongly aligned with your goal or road map. Every system responds to the goals and purpose of the business. The alignment of your business goals to a specific purpose will define the workability of the system you create and the amount of leverage you can multiply from it; corresponding to guarantee your residual income and wealth.

The returns from business far overweight and compensate greatly than the other three vehicles of wealth creation, business leverages time and multiplies your value with unlimited rewards. You can as well add the leverage of technology in real-time to monitor and leverage your business where you are anywhere in the world.

About the book

The magnificent keys to personal success identify and validate the fundamental path to a guaranteed future. It explored a dimensional approach to purpose, reveal for laws of money, and showcase how time and opportunities can be utilized to get satisfaction, fulfillment, mattering, self-actualization, and overall success. It is a quick manual for recovering our lives and giving meaning to existence. Purpose, determination, money, and time are linked together as an easy strategy to get success. Now you know more than is required to achieve success.

www.ingramcontent.com/pod-product-compliance
Lightning Source LLC
LaVergne TN
LVHW050333160826
845677LV00014B/3607

9798352213940